THE SWISS TWINS

By Lucy Fitch Perkins

ILLUSTRATED BY THE AUTHOR

HOUGHTON MIFFLIN COMPANY
BOSTON   NEW YORK   CHICAGO   SAN FRANCISCO
The Riverside Press Cambridge

By Lucy Fitch Perkins

Geographical Series

THE DUTCH TWINS PRIMER. *Grade I.*
THE ESKIMO TWINS. *Grade II.*
THE DUTCH TWINS. *Grade III.*
THE FILIPINO TWINS. *Grade IV.*
THE JAPANESE TWINS. *Grade IV.*
THE SWISS TWINS. *Grade IV.*
THE IRISH TWINS. *Grade V.*
THE ITALIAN TWINS. *Grade V.*
THE SCOTCH TWINS. *Grade VI.*
THE MEXICAN TWINS. *Grade VI.*
THE BELGIAN TWINS. *Grade VII.*
THE FRENCH TWINS. *Grade VII.*

Historical Series

THE CAVE TWINS. *Grade IV.*
THE SPARTAN TWINS. *Grade V.*
THE COLONIAL TWINS OF VIRGINIA. *Grade VI.*
THE AMERICAN TWINS OF 1812. *Grade VI.*
THE PURITAN TWINS. *Grade VII.*

Each volume is illustrated by the author

HOUGHTON MIFFLIN COMPANY

COPYRIGHT, 1922, BY LUCY FITCH PERKINS

ALL RIGHTS RESERVED

The Riverside Press
CAMBRIDGE · MASSACHUSETTS
PRINTED IN THE U.S.A.

CONTENTS

I. The Responsible Cuckoo	1
II. The Twins learn a New Trade	17
III. A Mountain Storm	37
IV. The Lonely Herdsman	65
V. The Pass	85
VI. New Friends and Old	117
Suggestions to Teachers	133

This book belongs to

I
THE RESPONSIBLE CUCKOO

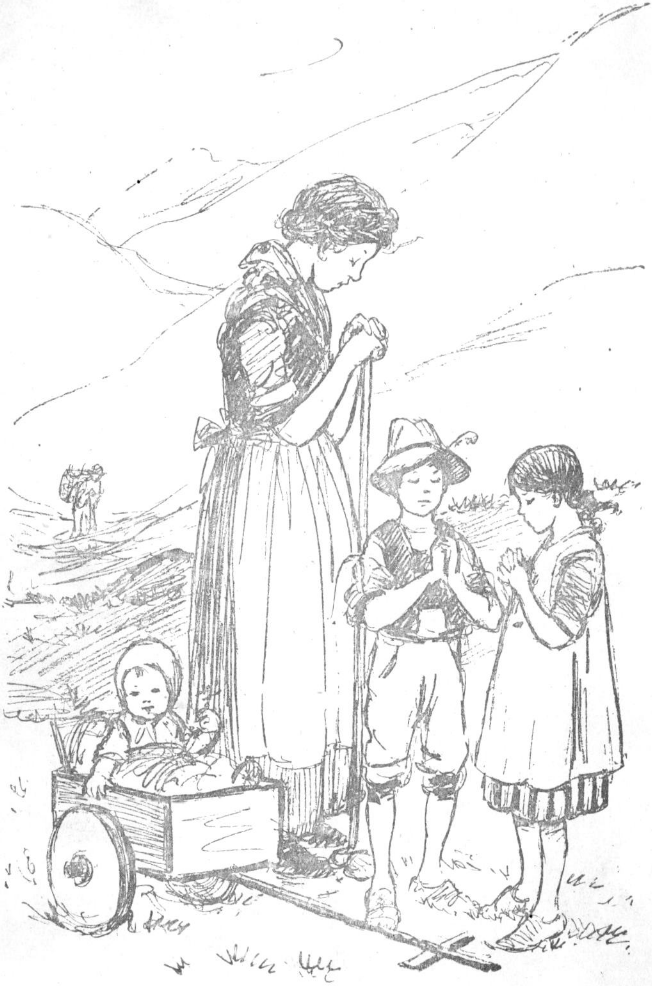

I

THE RESPONSIBLE CUCKOO

High on the kitchen wall of an old farmhouse on a mountain-side in Switzerland there hangs a tiny wooden clock. In the tiny wooden clock there lives a tiny wooden cuckoo, and every hour he hops out of his tiny wooden door, takes a look about to see what is going on in the world, shouts out the time of day, and pops back again into his little dark house, there to wait and tick away the minutes until it is time once more to tell the hour.

Late one spring afternoon, just as the sun was sinking out of sight, lighting up the snow-capped mountains with beautiful colors and sending long shafts of golden light across the valleys, the cuckoo woke with a start.

"Bless me!" he said to himself. "Here it is six o'clock and not a sound in the kitchen! It's high time for Mother Adolf to be getting supper. What in the world this family would do without me I really cannot think! They'd never know it was supper time if I did n't tell them, and would starve to death as likely as not. It is lucky for them I am such a responsible bird." The tiny wooden door flew open and he stuck out his tiny wooden head. There was not a sound in the kitchen but the loud ticking of the clock.

"Just as I thought," said the cuckoo. "Not a soul here."

There stood the table against the kitchen wall, with a little gray mouse on it nibbling a crumb of cheese. A long finger of sunlight streamed through the western window and touched the great stone stove, as if trying to waken the fire within. A beam fell upon a pan of water standing on the floor and sent gay sparkles of light dancing over the shining tins in the cupboard. The cuckoo saw it all at a glance. "This will never do," he ticked indignantly. There was a queer rumbling sound in his insides as if his feelings were getting quite too much for him, and then suddenly he sent a loud "cuckoo" ringing through the silent room. Instantly the little gray mouse leaped down from the table and scampered away to his hole in the wall, the golden sunbeam flickered and was gone, and shadows began to creep into the corners. "Cuckoo, cuckoo," he shouted at the top of his voice, "cuckoo, cuckoo, cuckoo," — six times in all, — and then, his duty done, he popped back again into his little dark house, and the door clicked behind him.

Out in the garden Mother Adolf heard him and, raising her head from the onion-bed, where she was pulling weeds, she counted on her fingers, "One, two, three, four, five, six! Bless my soul, six o'clock and the sun already out of sight behind old Pilatus," she said, and, rising from her knees a little stiffly, she stood for a moment looking down the green slopes toward the valley.

Far, far below, the blue waters of Lake Lucerne mirrored the glowing colors of the mountain-peaks beyond its farther shore, and nearer, among the foothills of old Pilatus itself, a little village nestled among green trees, its roofs clustered about a white church-spire. Now the bells in the steeple began to ring, and the sound floated out across the green fields spangled with yellow daffodils, and reached Mother Adolf where she stood. Bells from more distant villages soon joined in the clamor, until all the air was filled with music and a hundred echoes woke in the mountains.

The tiny wooden cuckoo heard them and ticked loudly with satisfaction. "Everybody follows me," he said to himself proudly. "I wake all the bells in the world."

"Where can the children be?" said Mother Adolf aloud to herself, looking about the garden. "I have n't heard a sound from either the baby or the Twins for over an hour," and, making a hollow between her hands, she added her own bit of music to the chorus of the hills.

she sang, and immediately from behind the willows which fringed the brook at the end of the garden two childish voices gave back an answering strain.

A moment later two sunburned, tow-headed, blue-eyed children, a boy and girl of ten, appeared, dragging after them a box mounted on rough wooden wheels in which there sat a round, pink, blue-eyed cherub of a baby. Shouting with laughter, they came tearing up the garden path to their mother's side.

"Hush, my children," said Mother Adolf, laying her finger on her lips. "It is the Angelus."

The shouts were instantly silenced, and the two children stood beside the mother with clasped hands and bowed heads until the echoes of the bells died away in the distance.

Far down on the long path to the village a man, bending under the weight of a huge basket, also stood still for a moment in silent prayer, then toiled again up the steep slope.

"See," cried Mother Adolf as she lifted her head, "there comes Father from the village with bread for our supper in his basket. Run, Seppi, and help him bring the bundles home. Our Fritz will soon be coming with the goats, too, and he and Father will both be as hungry as wolves and in a hurry for their supper. Hark!" she paused to listen.

Far away from out the blue shadows of the mountain came the sound of a horn playing a merry little tune.

"There's Fritz now," cried Mother Adolf. "Hurry, Seppi, and you, Leneli, come with me to the kitchen. You can give little Roseli her supper, while I spread the table and set the soup to boil before the goats get here to be milked." She lifted the baby in her arms as she spoke, and set off at a smart pace toward the house, followed by Leneli dragging the cart and playing peek-a-boo with the baby over her mother's shoulder.

When they reached the door, Leneli sat down on the step, and Mother Adolf put the baby in her arms and went at once into the quiet house. Then there was a sound of quick steps about the kitchen, a rattling of the stove, and a clatter of tins which must have pleased the cuckoo, and soon she reappeared in the door with a bowl and spoon in her hands.

The bowl she gave to Leneli, and little Roseli, crowing with delight, seized the spoon and stuck it first into an eye, and then into her tiny pink button of a nose, in a frantic effort to find her mouth. It was astonishing to Baby Roseli how that rosebud mouth of hers managed to hide itself, even though she was careful to keep it wide open while she searched for it. When she had explored her whole face with the spoon in vain, Leneli took the tiny hand in hers and guided each mouthful down the little red lane.

Over their heads the robin in the cherry tree by the door sat high up on a twig and chirped a good-night song to his nestlings. "Cherries are ripe, cherries are ripe, cherries are ripe in June," sang the robin. At least that is what Leneli told the baby he said, and surely she ought to know.

Before Baby Roseli had finished the last mouthful of her supper, Father and Seppi appeared with the bundles, and then there was the clatter of many little hoofs on the hard earth of the door-yard, and round the corner of the old gray farm-house came big brother Fritz with the goats. With Fritz came Bello, his faithful dog, barking and wagging his tail for joy at getting home again. Bello ran at once to Leneli and licked her hand, nearly upsetting the bowl of milk in his noisy greeting, and the baby crowed with delight and seized him by his long, silky ears.

"Down, Bello, down," cried Leneli, holding the bowl high out of reach; "you'll spill the baby's supper!" And Bello, thinking she meant that he should beg for it, sat up on his hind legs with his front paws crossed and barked three times, as Fritz had taught him to do.

"He must have a bite or he'll forget his manners," laughed Fritz, and Leneli broke off a crumb of bread and tossed it to him. Bello caught it before it fell, swallowed it at one gulp, and begged for more.

"No, no," said Leneli, "good old Bello, go now with Fritz and help him drive the goats to the milking-shed, and by and by you shall have your supper."

Fritz whistled, and instantly Bello was off like a shot after Nanni, the brown goat, who was already on her way to the garden to eat the young green carrot-tops she saw peeping out of the ground.

"It's time that child was in bed," said the cuckoo to himself, and out he came from his little house and called "cuckoo" seven times so reproachfully that Leneli hastened upstairs with the baby and put her down in her crib at once.

Baby Roseli did not agree with the cuckoo. She wanted to stay up and play with Bello, and hear the robin sing, but Leneli sat down beside the crib, and while Mother Adolf milked the goats she sang over and over again an old song.

"Sleep, baby, sleep!
 Thy father watches the sheep,
 Thy mother is shaking the dreamland tree
 And down falls a little dream on thee.
 Sleep, baby, sleep!"

"Sleep, baby, sleep!
 The large stars are the sheep,
 The little stars are the lambs, I guess,
 And the silver moon is the shepherdess.
 Sleep, baby, sleep!"

Over and over she sang it, until at last the heavy lids closed over the blue eyes. Then she crept quietly down the creaking stairs in the dark, and ate her bread and cheese and drank her soup by candle-light with her father and mother, Seppi and Fritz, all seated about the kitchen table.

By nine o'clock the room was once more silent and deserted, the little mouse was creeping quietly from his hole in the wall, and Bello lay by the door asleep with his nose on his paws. High over Mt. Pilatus the moon sailed through the star-lit sky, bathing the old gray farm-house in silver light and playing hide and seek with shadows on the snow-capped peaks.

"Cuckoo," called the tiny wooden cuckoo nine times, and at once the bells in the village steeple answered him. "That's as it should be," ticked the cuckoo. "That church-bell is really very intelligent. Let me see; to-morrow morning I must wake the roosters at three, and the sun at four, and the family must be up by five. I'll just turn in and get a wink of sleep myself while I can," and he popped into the clock once more and shut the door.

II
THE TWINS LEARN A NEW TRADE

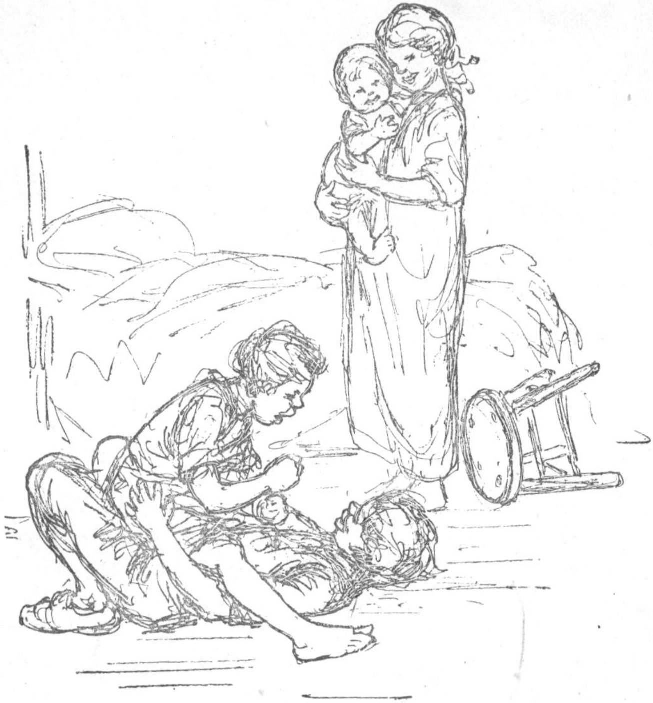

II

THE TWINS LEARN A NEW TRADE

At five o'clock the next morning Father and Mother Adolf were already up, and the cuckoo woke Fritz, but though he shouted five times with all his might and main, neither Seppi nor Leneli stirred in their sleep.

"Fritz, go wake the Twins," said Mother Adolf, when he came to the door of the shed where she was milking the goats. "Only don't wake the baby. I want her to sleep as long as she will."

"Yes, Mother," said Fritz dutifully, and he was off at once, leaping up the creaky stairs three steps at a time.

He went first to Leneli's bed and tickled her toes. She drew up her knees and slept on. Then he went to Seppi's bed, and when shaking and rolling over failed to rouse him, he took him by one leg and pulled him out of bed. Seppi woke up with a roar and cast himself upon Fritz, and in a moment the two boys were rolling about on the floor, yelling like Indians. The uproar woke Leneli, and the baby too, and Mother Adolf, hearing the noise, came running from the goat-shed just in time to find Seppi sitting on top of Fritz beating time on his stomach to a tune which he was singing at the top of his lungs. The baby was crowing with delight as she watched the scuffle from Leneli's arms.

Mother Adolf gazed upon this lively scene with dismay. Then she picked Seppi off Fritz's stomach and gazed sternly at her oldest son. "Fritz," said she, "I told you to be quiet and not wake the baby."

"I was quiet," said Fritz, sitting up. "I was just as quiet as I could be, but they wouldn't wake up that way, so I had to pull Seppi out of bed; there was no other way to get him up." He looked up at his mother with such honest eyes that in spite of herself her lips twitched and then she smiled outright.

"I should have known better than to send such a great overgrown pup of a boy as you on such an errand," she said. "Bello would have done it better. Next time I shall send him.

"And now, since you are all awake, I will tell you the great news that Father told me last night. He has been chosen by the commune to take the herds of the village up to the high alps to be gone all summer. He will take Fritz with him to guard the cattle while he makes the cheese. There is no better cheese-maker in all the mountains than your father, and that is why the commune chose him," she finished proudly.

More than anything else in the world, every boy in that part of Switzerland longs to go with the herds to the high mountain pastures for the summer, and Fritz was so delighted that he turned a somersault at once to express his feelings. When he was right side up again, a puzzled look came over his face, and he said, "Who will take care of our own goats?"

"Ah," answered his mother, and she sighed a little. "There is no one but Seppi and Leneli. Together they must fill your place, and you, Fritz, must take them with you to-day up the mountain to learn the way and begin their work."

"To-day! This very day?" screamed the Twins. They had never been up to the goat-pastures in their lives, and it was a most exciting event.

Then Leneli thought of her mother. She flung her arms about her neck. "But who will stay with you, dear Mother?" she cried. "All day you will be alone, with everything to do and no one to speak to but the baby."

"Yes," sighed the mother, "that is true. It will be a long, lonely summer for me, but there is no other way, so we must each do our part bravely and not complain. It is good fortune that Father and Fritz will both be earning money in the alps, and, with wise old Bello to help you, you will soon be as good goatherds as your brother. Come, now, hurry and eat your breakfasts, for the goats are already milked and impatient to be gone."

She took Roseli in her arms and disappeared down the stairs, and when, a few moments later, the Twins and Fritz came into the kitchen, she had their breakfast of bread and milk ready for them, and their luncheon of bread and cheese wrapped in a clean white cloth for Fritz to put in his pocket.

Father Adolf came back from the garden, where he had been hoeing potatoes, to see the little procession start away for the hills. First came the goats, frisking about in the fresh morning air and jingling all their bells. Then came Bello, looking very important, then Fritz with a cock's feather in his cap and his little horn and his cup slung over his shoulder, and last of all the Twins.

"It's a long way, my children," said Mother Adolf, as she kissed them goodbye. "Your legs will get tired, but you must climb on just the same. If every one stopped when he was tired, the world's work would never be done. Learn the way carefully and remember always to pray if any danger comes. You are very near the good God on the mountain, and He will take care of you if you ask Him, never fear."

"Obey Fritz," said Father Adolf, "and do not stray off by yourselves. Stay always with Fritz and the goats."

"We will," cried the Twins, and away they ran to join their brother, who was already some little distance ahead of them. They turned as the path rounded the great cliff where the echoes lived, and the Twins waved their hands, while Fritz played his merry little tune on the horn. Then the rocks hid them from view, and the long climb began in earnest.

It was many rough uphill miles to the alps where the goats were pastured, and the stout little legs ached with weariness long before they reached the patches of green grass which were reserved for them. On the way up they passed fields where cows were grazing, and Bello had hard work to keep the goats in the path, but these pastures were only for cows, and goats were not allowed in them. For two hours they climbed steadily up and up, following a mountain path that led sometimes beside a rushing brook, sometimes along the edges of dizzy precipices, and always among rocks with wonderful views of distant snow-capped peaks above them and green, green valleys below.

At last, when it seemed to the weary children that they could not go another step, they came out upon a high pasture, where Fritz called a halt. The goats leaped joyfully forward, snatching greedy mouthfuls of the rich green grass which grew among the rocks. Bello flopped heavily down on a flat stone with his tongue hanging out, and Fritz and the Twins rolled over on their backs on a soft carpet of grass to rest.

Almost at once Seppi said, "I'm hungry."

"So 'm I," said Leneli.

"You'll be hungry all the time up here," said Fritz encouragingly. "It's the air."

"Let's eat," urged Seppi.

Fritz took the package of luncheon from his pocket and opened it.

"It looks very small. It looks a great deal smaller than it did at home," said Leneli. "I wonder why?"

"You are hungrier now than you were then," said Fritz.

"I could eat it all myself," said Seppi.

"But you won't," laughed Fritz; "I'll see to that." He divided the bread and cheese into three equal portions and handed one to each of the Twins. The third he put in his own pocket. "Now I don't care what you do with yours," he said; "only, if you eat it all now, you'll be hungry enough to browse with the goats before it's time to go home. Better take just a bite and a drink of water and eat more by and by."

Seppi looked hungrily at his portion and took a bite. Then he just couldn't stop, and before he knew it his whole luncheon was gone and it was only nine o'clock in the morning!

Leneli took two bites of hers, and then, wrapping it carefully in the piece of cloth, placed it high up on an overhanging rock out of the way of temptation. Then, while Fritz was teaching Seppi all the tricks of a goat-boy's trade, she found a soft patch of grass all spangled with blue gentians and fell asleep with her head on her arm. She slept for some time, and Fritz and Seppi, seeing how tired she was, did not disturb her.

She was roused at last by the tinkling of a goat-bell almost over her head, and woke up just in time to see her luncheon, cloth and all, disappearing into the mouth of Nanni, the brown goat! Poor Leneli screamed with dismay, and Fritz and Seppi, thinking perhaps she had hurt herself, came dashing to her side. Leneli was boiling with rage. She could only point at Nanni, who stood calmly out of reach above them with the last scrap of cloth dangling from her lips.

"You wretched, black-hearted pig of a goat!" she screamed, stamping her foot. "You 've eaten every bit of my lunch, and I 'd only taken two little teeny bites! Oh,

I wish I'd eaten it all like that greedy Seppi!"

Fritz and Seppi were sorry, but when they saw the goat looking down at Leneli so calmly while she stormed and scolded below, they rolled over on the ground helpless with laughter.

"It's all very well for you to laugh," sniffed Leneli; "you've both got your lunches," and she went away quite sulkily and sat down on a stone by herself. Bello came and sat beside her and licked her hand.

Fritz had to dash away just then after a straying goat, but he was soon back again with his luncheon in his hand. "Here," he said, "you can have some of my bread and cheese."

"Oh, Fritzi," said Leneli gratefully, "you are as good and kind as that goat is bad, but I'm going to take only a teeny mouthful, just to keep me from starving!"

"All right," said Fritz, holding the slice of bread for her to bite. "To-morrow we'll ask Mother to put up more bread and cheese, and if you get hungry again, you can milk old Nanni herself and get even with her that way."

"But I don't know how to milk," said Leneli with her mouth full.

"It's time you learned then," said Fritz briskly. "You've seen Mother do it over and over again. Come, I'll teach you."

Nanni, the goat, had leaped down from her high perch, and was now taking a drink from a little sparkling mountain rill which flowed through the pasture.

"Come along," said Fritz. "There's no time like the present," and, taking his cup in his hand, he started toward her.

Leneli hung back a little. "Nanni is the naughtiest goat in the whole flock," she said resentfully. "If it were n't for getting my lunch back, I would n't try to milk her."

It may be that Nanni heard it and was offended, or it may be that she knew that she had no milk to give them so early in the morning. Anyway, she made up her mind she would not be bothered at that time of day, so as fast as they came near her, she walked on a few steps, and by the time they had reached that spot she had moved farther still.

"We must n't frighten her," said Fritz. "It's bad for the milk."

For some time they patiently followed her about, and at last just as they were ready to lay hands upon her, she suddenly leaped upon a rock and from that to a higher one, until she stood far out of reach on a dizzy overhanging cliff.

"That Nanni!" cried Fritz wrathfully as he prepared to follow her. "She'll break her pesky neck and mine too some day."

He climbed a tree for a short cut to the cliff and dropped from an overhanging branch to the narrow shelf of rock in front of the goat. Bello, meanwhile, ran back and forth below, barking like everything, but quite unable either to follow Nanni up the steep trail, or to climb the tree as Fritz had done.

"Come, Nanni," said Fritz, holding out his hand as he stepped carefully toward her.

Nanni sniffed and backed. Leneli and Seppi watched from below, breathless with anxiety. If she should back too much she might fall over the cliff and be killed. If she should dash forward she might knock Fritz over it instead. But Fritz was a wise goat-boy! He put his hand in his pocket and drew out a handful of salt, which he kept for just such times as this. He held it out toward Nanni and carefully and slowly backed away from the edge of the cliff, coaxing her to follow him. As she stepped forward, he stepped back, and in this way led her by a roundabout path down the farther side of the rocks to the place where the other goats were still feeding.

"Oh, Fritzi, I never could do that," said Leneli, hugging him when he was on safe ground once more. "I should be so frightened."

"I could," said Seppi promptly; "I'm not afraid."

"Don't you try it, young man," said Fritz, "unless it's the only thing you can do. The best goat-boy is the one who keeps his goats from getting into such places. It's much cleverer to keep out of trouble than to get out."

They gave up the milking lesson for the time being, but when the long day was over and they were on their way down the mountain-pass in the late afternoon, they came to a wide level space. Here they paused, and, while Seppi stood with his arm about Nanni's neck and fed her handfuls of green grass, Leneli really did milk enough for a refreshing drink to sustain her on the long homeward journey.

Singing, playing tunes on the horn, and rousing the ever-ready echoes with their yodels, they ran down the steep mountain path in a much shorter time than it had taken to climb it in the morning, and came in sight of the old farm-house just as the Angelus rang again in the little white village spire. They paused on the mountain path and bent their heads, but Nanni was not a religious goat! She remembered the glimpse she had had the night before of green things growing in the garden and suddenly bolted down the steep path at a break-neck speed. All the rest of the flock followed pell-mell after her, and the children were obliged to cut short their prayers in order to save the carrot-tops from being eaten up.

The last mile was covered in record-breaking time, and before the cuckoo clock struck seven the children and goats and dog all came galloping into the yard together.

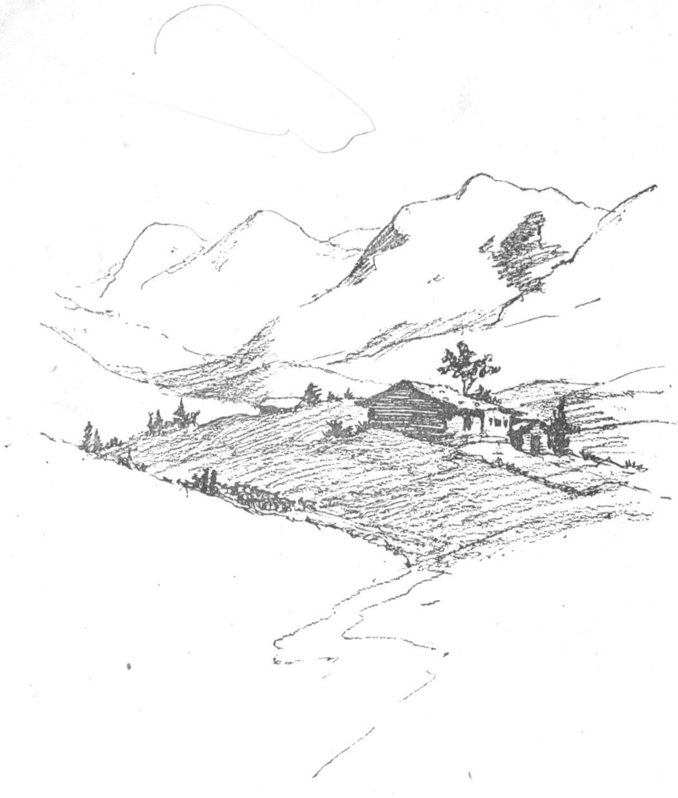

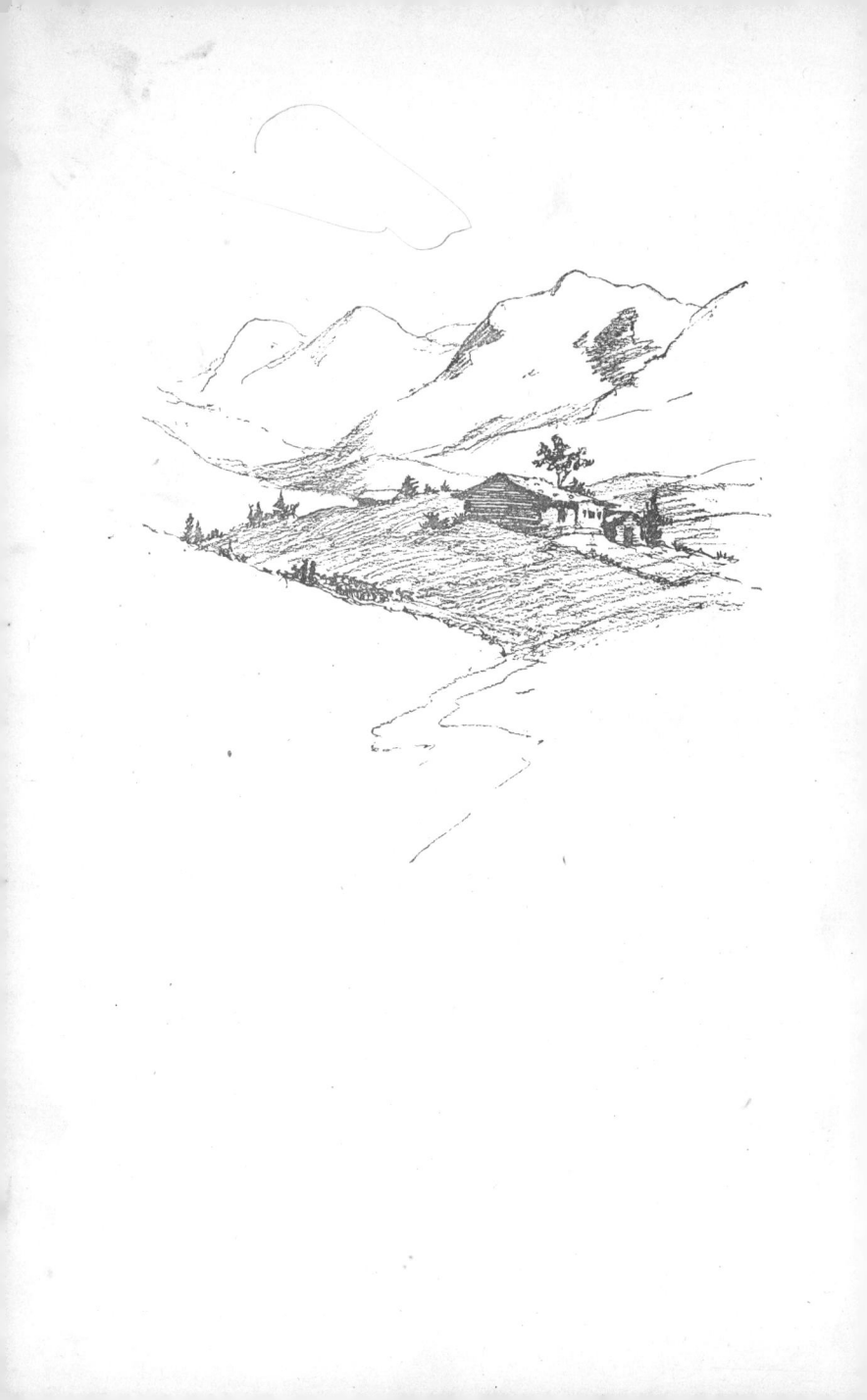

III
A MOUNTAIN STORM

III

A MOUNTAIN STORM

The next day, and the day after that, the same lesson was repeated. The Twins went away with Fritz in the early morning and stayed all day long with the goats and came home with him in the sunset glow. But on the fourth day it was quite, quite different. It was different not only because they were to go alone with the goats for the first time, but also because it was the day when the greatest event of the whole year was to happen.

On that very morning the cattle were to start away to the high alps to be gone all summer! Every one in the little gray farmhouse was up with the dawn, and while Mother Adolf milked the goats, the Twins took their breakfast to a high rock beside the mountain path, where they could get a good view of the village below. Father Adolf and Fritz had kissed Mother Adolf and the baby good-bye before daylight, and had gone to the village to get the cattle in line for their long march. They did not say good-bye to the Twins, for they were to join the procession when it passed the house, since for the first two miles the paths to the high alps where the cattle grazed and to the goat-pastures were the same.

Leneli and Seppi had finished their bread and milk and were hopping about in great excitement on the hill-top, when suddenly from the village below there was a burst of gay music and they knew that the procession had begun to move. Seppi ran back to the milking-shed as fast as his legs could carry him. "They're coming, they're coming!" he shouted.

"Our goats are ready," said Mother Adolf. "You and Bello may take them out to the path and wait there until the cattle

have passed by. Then you must fall in behind them with Father and Fritz and go with them as far as the Giant Pine Tree that stands at the parting of the paths. Father and Fritz will leave you there, and you and Leneli must go on alone. You are sure you know the way?" She looked anxiously into Seppi's blue eyes.

"Oh, yes, Mother," said Seppi, confidently. "Don't you worry. I know it well, and so does Leneli. We can take care of the goats just as well as Fritz. You'll see!"

Seppi, with Bello's help, drove the goats to a place where they could crop the grass beside the mountain path, and there a few moments later Mother Adolf joined them, dragging the baby in the wooden cart. The procession was already in plain sight, winding up the steep mountain path from the village. First came three fine brindled cows, each with a bell as big as a bucket hanging from her neck and a wreath of flowers about her horns. After them came thirty more, each with a smaller bell, marching proudly along in single file behind the leaders. All the bells were jingling, and all the people who followed them from the village were singing and yodeling until the air was full of jolly sounds. The last cow in line carried the milking-stool on her horns, and behind her walked Father and Fritz.

Bello, who understood very well what was going on, kept the goats herded together beside the path, and when Seppi and Leneli, singing and shouting with the rest, drove them forward, Bello marched proudly right behind the goats, barking and waving his tail like a flag.

Mother Adolf's heart swelled with pride as she watched her husband and children march away so gayly, but when they had disappeared from view and the music sounded fainter and fainter as it grew more distant, she wiped her eyes on her apron, picked up the Twins' breakfast-bowls, and went slowly with little Roseli back to the lonely farm-house. The people from the village walked but a little way up the mountain-side, and when they too returned to their homes, there were no more songs and yodels, and a great silence settled over the mountain.

Up and up the rocky trail wound the long train of cattle and goats, until they came to the Giant Pine Tree, and here Father Adolf and Fritz stopped.

"Remember, my children," said Father Adolf solemnly to the Twins, "the goats are our only wealth. If they stray away and are lost or fall over a cliff and are killed, the fault will be yours. You must be faithful, watchful, and brave, and let nothing happen to the goats lest we go hungry when winter comes." Then he and Fritz said good-bye, and the children, feeling very solemn and important, went on their lonely way.

Bello was a wonderful dog. He could count, for he always knew when one of the goats was missing and would run about with his nose to the trail until he found her, then he would bark at her heels until she came back to join the flock. But, clever as he was, he was puzzled when he saw the goats going in one direction and Fritz in another. He stood at the parting of the paths and looked first one way, then the other, and whined; then he dashed after Fritz.

"No, no, Bello, go with the goats," cried Fritz. Bello's ears and tail drooped, and he looked pleadingly up at Fritz.

Fritz had given his little horn to Seppi, and now he shouted to him, "Blow your horn." Seppi could not play Fritz's merry little tune, but he blew a terrific blast, and Bello knew that he must follow the sound of the horn, even though it meant parting from his dear Fritz.

"Good old dog!" said Fritz, patting him; "go find them," and Bello licked his hand, then tore away up the mountain after the goats.

When he reached them, he tried to round them up and drive them back to Fritz, and it was some time before Seppi could make him understand that the goats must go to the pastures as usual. Then, though he followed them faithfully, he did not run about in circles and bark down every hollow log as he usually did. Instead, he walked along solemnly beside Leneli with his nose in her hand.

"See, Seppi," she said, "he knows he must help with the goats, but he wants to go with Fritz."

"There are lots of people in the world that know less than Bello," Seppi answered wisely. He put the horn to his lips, puffed out his cheeks, and blew with all his might. It made a fearful noise, which was echoed from all the surrounding cliffs and was answered by Fritz's yodel far away on the mountain path. Bello pricked up his ears and whined. They called back and forth in this way, the sounds growing fainter and fainter in the distance, until they could no longer hear each other at all, and the Twins were for the first time quite alone on the mountain with Bello and the goats.

When at last they reached the pasture, they threw themselves down on the grass, and Leneli at once took her knitting out of her pocket and went to work. Bello sighed

and lay down beside her, with his eyes on the goats. The sun was warm and it was very still on the mountain-side. There was no sound except the tearing noise made by the goats as they cropped the grass and the tinkle of their bells. Then Seppi began to practice on his horn. He blew and blew until he was red in the face, trying to play Fritz's tune, but only a hoarse bellow came from its throat.

Leneli stood the noise for some time. Then she plucked a blade of grass, stretched it across a hollow between her two thumbs, and, when Seppi was not looking, blew with all her might right by his ear! It made a fearful screech, which echoed and reëchoed until it seemed as if the very air had been broken into a million bits.

Seppi gave a screech of his own and clapped his hands over his ears. "What did you do that for?" he said crossly, "just when I was beginning to get the tune."

"Well," said Leneli, "you may have begun, but you were still a long, long way from getting it! My noise was just as good as yours! I'll stop if you will."

Seppi grumpily laid aside his horn and sat hugging his knees and looking at the wonderful view spread out before them. Across the valley the Rigi lifted its crest

to the sky. Little toy villages, each with its white spire, lay sleeping silently in the sunshine. On the shores of the lake far below he could see the city of Lucerne. It might have been a painted city, for not a sound reached them from its busy streets, and there was no movement to be seen except here and there the waving of a tiny thread of smoke. On the lake the white sails looked, at that distance, like tiny white butterflies hovering over the blue water.

"I suppose we can see almost the whole world from here; don't you?" said Leneli.

"Pooh! no," Seppi answered loftily. "There's lots more to it than this, though this is the best part of it, of course. Why, there are oceans bigger than Lake Lucerne and a mile deep, and there's Paris and London besides."

"Dear, dear," said Leneli. "Mother says we are very near to God on the mountains, and I suppose He can look down and see everybody and know just what they are doing all the time, but I don't see how He possibly can keep track of all of us at once."

"He can't, silly," answered her brother, still more loftily. "Don't you know that the earth is round, so He can't see but one side at a time, if He looks ever so hard? I suppose that's why He made the night-time.

He shuts some of the people up in the dark while He watches the rest of them on the other side." Seppi had never thought this out before, but he always tried to have some answer to give to Leneli when she asked questions, or else she might get the idea that he did n't know any more than she did. Leneli usually believed whatever he told her, and, this question being settled, she went on with her knitting.

The goats grazed peacefully about them; the air was very still and grew quite warm in the sunshine. About the snow-white crest of the Rigi little wisps of clouds were gathering. They grew longer and longer and sank lower on the mountain-side.

"It's raining in Lucerne," said Seppi.

The clouds fell still lower and spread over the whole valley, until the children from their high seat looked out over a sea of mist. There were sounds of distant thunder from the rolling clouds and vivid flashes of lightning far below them.

"It's a little lonesome up here with all

the world shut away out of sight, and nobody around but God; is n't it?" said Leneli timidly.

"There are the goats, and Bello," answered Seppi comfortingly. He looked straight up into the sky. Little wisps of clouds were gathering around the crest of old Pilatus now. The sun was suddenly hidden, and he felt a drop of rain. "It's going to rain here in a minute, and hard, too," he said.

"What shall we do?" cried Leneli, rolling up her knitting and springing to her feet.

"Get wet, I guess," answered Seppi. "There's no shelter."

"There must be something," said Leneli. "I'll look, while you and Bello get the goats together." She dashed away as she spoke, and soon from a point farther down the mountain they heard her call.

Goats, Bello, and Seppi, all came thundering down the path together and found her huddled under an overhanging rock, sheltered by the branches of a spreading pine. Bello and Seppi dived under the rock beside her, and the goats gathered close about them just as the storm broke in earnest. The lightning flashed, the thunder rolled, and the rain came down in torrents, making a gray curtain of water about the rock. The children shrank back under the shelter as far as they could go, and neither one said a word, except once when a stream of water suddenly ran down the back of Leneli's neck. Then she jumped and said "Ow," in a voice that Seppi heard even above the roar of the thunder.

For a long time they sat there while the storm raged about them. Then the thunder went roaring away farther and farther down the valley, the rain ceased, and the sun came out.

"The storm's over," said Seppi. "Let's get out of here."

The goats had already scattered and were nibbling tufts of wet grass, when the two children crawled out from under the rock.

Leneli's dress was quite muddy where the rain had come through the crack and poured down her neck, and she was twisting herself round, trying to see the extent of the damage, when suddenly there was a terrific roar and rumble as if the thunder had begun all over again, though the sky was blue and clear. Crash followed crash, and there was a sound of great rocks falling from dizzy mountain-heights far above them.

The children clung to each other in terror, the goats trembled, and Bello crept farther under the rock. "The avalanche!" gasped Leneli, shaking with fright. "Father thought there would n't be any more this spring! Oh, I wish we were home!"

Far down the mountain-side there were sounds of mighty trees being torn up by the roots and of rocks broken from the cliffs and bounding from ledge to ledge.

It seemed as if the whole world were being torn to pieces. At last the terrible roar ceased and a terrible silence settled over the mountains. The children knew well the awful dangers of the avalanche. Ever since they could remember they had heard stories of travelers buried alive under masses of snow and ice, and of whole villages swept away, or so covered with stones, trees, and earth that not a sign of them was ever seen again.

Their first thought was of their mother.

"Oh," shuddered Leneli, "do you suppose our house was in the path of it?"

Seppi thought a moment; then he said soberly, "No, that could n't be, for there is a wide hollow between our farm and the mountain-slope that would have to be filled first. I'm quite sure no avalanche could possibly carry the house away."

"Father—Fritz," sobbed Leneli.

"They are far round on the other side of the mountain by this time," said Seppi, "where the sun has not yet had so much chance to melt the snow and start avalanches. They could not have been harmed by this one, for it fell on our side of the mountain."

"Let us start home anyway," said Leneli, "even if it is early. I can't wait until night to know that Mother and Baby Roseli are safe."

"We ought to keep the goats up here eating all day," objected Seppi, "or they won't give any milk to-night."

"They may not give much anyway," answered Leneli, "because they've been so frightened, but we will let them go slowly and they can get a bite here and there as they go."

She took up her alpenstock, a long stick which she always carried with her, hung the little bundle of lunch, tied up in a cloth, from the end of it, put the stick over her shoulder, and, calling Bello, began at once to herd the goats together.

Seppi followed her a little doubtfully, and soon they were all on their way down the steep mountain path. The sun was now shining again as brilliantly as ever; the white clouds were floating lazily across the deep blue sky, and it did not seem as if anything unusual could possibly have happened.

Seppi's conscience troubled him. "It was only a thunder-storm after all," he said to Leneli, "and the avalanche is past and gone. It can't do any more harm. I'm afraid Father wouldn't like us to give up and go home now. He might think we were no better than babies to be so scared when we know we aren't hurt."

Leneli did not answer, but she kept right on going, and for a time they trudged along in silence. They had reached the Giant Pine where the trails divided, and had rounded a bend in the path, when Bello, who was a little way ahead with the goats, suddenly set up a furious barking.

"It's that Nanni, I do not doubt," said Seppi. "She's probably trying to break her neck somewhere." He dashed ahead and disappeared around a high rock, Leneli following him at a slower pace.

In a moment Seppi came running back to her, his face pale with surprise and alarm.

"It is n't Nanni," he gasped, "it 's the avalanche! It 's all across the pass! We can't get by."

He seized his sister's hand and dragged her to the top of the rock which overlooked the pass, and there they gazed in dismay at the scene before them. Where that morning the procession from the village had so gayly followed the winding trail up the mountain-side, there was now a great mass of rocks, ice, and snow completely blocking the path. Worse than that, the avalanche had made a dam across the bed of the mountain stream where the cattle stopped to drink, turning it into a little lake which was growing wider and deeper every moment. The goats were huddled together on the brink, bleating anxiously, while Bello, completely bewildered, ran back and forth, barking wildly.

The children knew well how serious their situation was; they were alone on the mountain, the only pass to the village closed, and without food except the lunch they had brought from home that morning. For a few moments they watched the water rising steadily in the little lake, too terrified to speak; then Leneli said, "Let's go back to the Giant Pine and think."

Seppi blew his little horn, but, instead of rounding up the goats, Bello only looked at him and whined. It had been a day of tremendous surprises to Bello. First Fritz had left him; then came the thunder-storm; then starting home in the middle of the day instead of at the proper time; and now the path itself was gone! No wonder he was bewildered. Seppi dashed down to the water's edge and drove the goats up the trail again himself, and while they snatched stray mouthfuls here and there about the pine tree, he and Leneli sat down under it to think.

"We can't get home that way; that's certain," said Seppi, pointing to the buried pass.

"And we can't stay here either," moaned Leneli; "not if there is a way out in any direction."

"There's the path Father and Fritz took this morning," said Seppi. "We might try that. It must go somewhere."

"Perhaps that is blocked too," said Leneli.

"I'll go a little way and see," said Seppi. "You stay here and watch the goats."

"Give me your horn, then," said Leneli,

"and I'll blow it every little while so you can find your way back. You know Father always tells us not to leave the path because it's so easy to get lost."

"That's a good idea," said Seppi. "See if you can blow it."

Leneli put it to her lips and blew until her face was purple, but achieved only a dismal squawk.

"I'll keep the horn myself," said Seppi, taking it from her, "and every little while I'll blow it. You can answer by blowing on a grass stem the way you did up yonder. Girls can't manage a horn anyway."

Leneli was too miserable to reply, and in another minute Seppi had disappeared up the strange path. For what seemed to her a very long time, Leneli answered the horn, as it grew fainter and fainter in the distance. Finally she could not hear it at all.

"Oh, what shall I do if Seppi's gone too?" she moaned when her desperate signals brought no answer.

Then her Mother's words came back to her, and, plumping herself down on her knees among the goats, she sent up a fervent prayer.

"Oh, dear God," she cried, clasping her hands, "Mother said we should be very close to you on the mountain and I suppose you can see me and Seppi both at the same time, from where you are. Please, please send him back for I'm scared. Dear God, do please hurry and help us find the way down the mountain before it gets dark and you have to go away to watch the other side of the world. Amen."

She rose from her knees and listened. Far away there came the sound of Seppi's horn. "Oh, thank you, God! There he comes!" she cried joyfully, and, snatching a grass-blade, she put it between her thumbs and gave an answering blast.

Soon Seppi himself came bounding into sight. "Come along," he shouted, waving his hand frantically toward the path, and Leneli at once called Bello, and together they started the goats.

"The avalanche must have begun on the other side of our pass," said Seppi when Leneli caught up with him. "There's no sign of it on this side."

"Maybe if we follow far enough we'll find Father and Fritz," said Leneli, brightening.

"I thought of that, too," answered Seppi, "but if there is any way to get down the mountain, I think we ought to do it on Mother's account. Father and Fritz won't know about it, so they won't be anxious, but if we don't get home Mother will think we are killed."

"Oh, I wish we could fly," said Leneli.

"Then we must wish for wings on the goats too," said Seppi, "for you know Father said we must take care of them whatever happens."

Sad and frightened though she was, Leneli giggled a little at that. "Wouldn't they look funny flying through the air with you and me and Bello all flopping after them?" she said. "Anyway, they might go a little faster than they do now," she added impatiently, giving Nanni a poke with her stick.

"They are hungry," said Seppi. "They hardly had time to eat anything before the storm came up."

Then a bright idea came into his head. "I'm hungry, too," he said, "and so are you. Let's eat our lunch while the goats get a few mouthfuls among the rocks, and then we shall all have more strength and shall get along faster."

IV
THE LONELY HERDSMAN

IV
THE LONELY HERDSMAN

The sun was already dipping toward the west when they finished the last crumb of their bread and cheese, washed it down with a drink from the mountain stream, and started once more on their journey. They followed the path without much difficulty, for it had been trampled by the feet of many cattle that morning, and at the end of an hour had covered several miles without meeting a person or finding any sign of human habitation. The way grew wilder and wilder and wound slowly upward.

"It's going to be dark pretty soon," said Leneli at last, trying hard to conceal the tremble in her voice, "and we are going up instead of down. Seppi, do you suppose there are any bears and wolves about here?"

"Maybe," said Seppi, and there was a little catch in his throat, too. "But then," he added, trying hard to look on the bright side of things, "if there are, they'd be much more likely to eat the goats. I don't believe they care much about eating people."

"Well, anyway, if they do," quavered Leneli, "I hope they'll begin with Nanni."

The afternoon waned; the shadows grew longer and longer, and they were just making up their minds that they must soon lie down among the goats beside the trail and wait for morning, when a turn in the path brought them out on a spur of the mountain where they could look for miles across a deep valley towards the west. On the farther side, range after range of snow-capped peaks gave back the golden glory of the sunset, and from somewhere came the sound of an Alpine horn playing the first few notes of the hymn "Praise Ye the Lord."

"The Angelus!" cried Leneli clasping her hands. "They can't hear the churchbells up here, so they blow the horns instead."

Far away across the valley another horn answered, then another and another, and the echoes took up the refrain until it seemed as if the hills themselves were singing.

Following eagerly the direction of the sound the children were overjoyed to see in the distance a lonely herdsman standing on a great rock overlooking the valley, his long Alpine horn in his hand, and his head bowed in prayer. Leneli and Seppi bowed their heads too, and it comforted them to think that their mother in the old farm-house, and Father and Fritz on the far-away alp, were all at that same moment praying too. It seemed to bring them near together in spite of the distance which separated them.

Their prayers said, the children hastened forward, driving the goats before them, and now the sound of cow-bells mingled with the tinkle of the bells on the goats. Another turn in the path revealed a green pasture where a herd of cows was grazing, and, just beyond, a rough shelter made of logs with the herdsman, still holding his horn, standing beside it. He was gazing in astonishment at the sight of two little children alone on the mountains at so late an hour. He was an old man, with a shaggy white beard, and strange kind eyes that seemed always looking for something that he could not find. Beside him, his ears pointed forward and his tail pointing back, was his dog. The dog was growling.

For an instant the children stood still, not quite daring to go nearer, but Bello, dear friendly old Bello, had no such fears.

He ran forward barking joyfully; the two dogs smelled each other, and then trotted back down the path together as if they had been friends since they were puppies.

The man followed at a slower pace. "What in the world are you doing up here on the mountains with your goats at this time o' day?" he said to the children.

The Twins told him their story, and he stood for a moment scratching his head, as if he were much puzzled to know what to do with them.

"Well," he said at length, "you can't get down the mountain to-night, that's certain; and you must be hungry enough to eat an ox roasted whole, that's certain too. And your goats are hungry into the bargain. Goats are n't allowed in this pasture, but they must n't starve either. Nothing is as it should be."

He scratched his head again, and Leneli, fearing he was going to turn them away, could not keep a large tear from rolling down her nose and splashing off her chin.

"There, there," said the old herdsman, comfortingly, "don't you cry, sissy. Things are n't so bad but that they might be worse. You can sleep in the hay up yonder," he jerked his thumb toward the hut, "and I 'll give you a bite to eat, and the goats will help themselves, I 've no manner of doubt."

"We can drink goat's milk," said Leneli timidly, "and you may have all we don't take."

"We 'll have to milk them first," said Seppi, "and we 've never done it before. Mother always does the milking."

"I know how," said Leneli proudly. "Don't you remember, Fritz taught me the day Nanni swallowed my lunch?"

"I 'll lend you a milk-pail," said the herdsman. "The cows were all milked some time ago."

He went back to the hut and soon reappeared with two pails, and as Leneli struggled with one goat he milked another, while Seppi fed both creatures with tufts of grass to keep them quiet. It was the first good grass the goats had seen since morning, and apparently they were determined to eat the pasture clean.

The herdsman looked at them anxiously and scratched his head again. "They certainly have healthy appetites," he said woefully; "they don't calculate to leave anything behind 'em but stones and gravel!"

The milking took some time and after it was done, the old man placed the sad and tired children on the bench beside his door, and while they ate the food he gave them and watched the moon rise over the mountains, he told them about his home in the village fifteen miles away at the foot of the pass, and about his wife and two grandchildren who lived there with him.

"The only thing you can do," he said, "is to go down the pass on this side of the mountain. You can spend the night at my house or at some farm-house on the way and it is only about ten miles back to your own village from the foot of the pass."

"But how can we find the way?" quavered poor Leneli.

The old man scratched his head, as he always did when he was puzzled, and finally said, "Well, I'm blest if I can tell you. It's a hard pass. I'd go with you, but I'm alone here and I can't leave the cows even for half a day. I'll start you right, the dog and the goats have some sense of their own, and the good God will guide you. Besides, Swiss boys and girls are never afraid."

"I'm a little afraid, I think," confessed Leneli. She looked at the moon and thought how it must be shining down on the old farm-house; and of her mother, who at that very moment must be frantic with fears for their safety; and of the long and perilous journey before they could see her again, and though she tried hard to swallow them, three little sobs slipped out.

The old man heard them. "Why, bless me, bless me," he said, rumpling his hair until it stood on end, "this will never do at all! Why, bless us, think of William Tell! Think of Peter, who lived long ago in your own Lucerne, and who saved the whole city! To take a little herd of goats down a strange pass is child's play compared with what he did; and he was only a boy like Seppi here, and I always thought girls were braver than boys."

Leneli sat up and sniffed resolutely. "I think — I'm almost sure — I'm going to be brave now," she said. "Tell us about Peter."

"Well, it was like this," said the herdsman. "Peter was a smart, likely lad enough, but nobody thought he was a hero. In fact, he never suspected it himself. You see, you can't tell whether you are one or not until something happens that calls for courage. Then if you do the right thing, whether you are afraid or not, you'll know you are one. Well, one summer night this Peter went out to have a swim in the lake, and when he crawled up on the bank to dress again, he was so tired he fell asleep. By and by he was wakened by voices and, opening his eyes, he saw five or six men creeping stealthily along the lake-shore.

"'Aha,' says Peter to himself, 'that's not the walk of honest men.'

"He got up on his elbow in the long grass and watched them without being seen. He saw many more men steal silently after the first group, and among them he recognized the Bailiff of Rothenburg, whom he knew to be an Austrian and the sworn enemy of Lucerne. He saw the men talk together and heard enough of what they said to be sure that danger threatened his beloved town. So when they moved on, he followed them, slipping along behind rocks and bushes, until suddenly they disappeared as if the earth had swallowed them. Peter groped about hunting for them until at last he saw a faint light shining from out a dark cavern among the rocks. Then, though he knew how dangerous it was, he followed the light and found himself in a long, dark tunnel."

"Oh," shuddered Leneli. "I could never be as brave as that. I don't like dark places."

"Peter knew that a tunnel ran underneath the walls of the town and that the other end of it opened by a trap-door into a stable in Lucerne," went on the old man without noticing Leneli's interruption, "and at once he saw that some traitor must have told the Austrians of this secret passage. He crept closer and closer to the group of men, until he was near enough to hear what they said. You may be sure his blood ran cold in his veins when he heard the voice of a man he knew, telling the Austrians just how best they could capture the town! He knew that terrible things would happen in Lucerne that night if the enemy ever reached the other end of the tunnel, and at once made up his mind that he must alarm the town. He dropped on his hands and knees and was beginning to crawl back toward the entrance, when he heard some one coming into the tunnel! He sprang to his feet and tried to run past, but the passage was narrow, and he was caught at once and dragged into the light."

"Oh! Oh!" gasped the Twins, breathless with excitement. "It sounds just like a bad dream."

"It was no dream," said the old herdsman, "for when the traitor, whose name was Jean de Malters, saw Peter, he was terribly angry. 'How did you come here,' he roared, in a voice that made the earth shake.

"'I was asleep on the bank and you woke me up, so I followed to see what was going on,' said Peter.

"'I don't believe you. Some one sent you to spy upon us,' said Jean de Malters, and he shook Peter. 'Who sent you?'

"'No one,' said Peter. 'I have told you the truth.'

"'You lie,' said his captor. 'I'll give you just two minutes to tell who sent you, and if you do not tell us then, you shall die!'

"Poor Peter thought of his home and his mother and father, and there never was a more homesick boy in the world than he was at that moment, but though he was terribly frightened, he did not say a single word.

"'He shall die, then,' said Jean de Malters, when the two minutes were up, and Peter had not spoken.

"One of the Austrians interfered. 'No,'

he said. 'It would be bad luck to begin the night's work by shedding the blood of a child. Make him swear he will not tell what he has seen to any living soul, and let him go.'

"In spite of Jean de Malters, who was bound that he should be killed, that was what they did, and the moment he was free you may be sure Peter ran like the wind for home.

"Now you see," said the old herdsman, and he shook his finger at Seppi and Leneli, "this was a dreadful position for Peter. He had solemnly promised not to tell a living soul what he had seen and heard, but if he did n't tell, his parents and friends would be murdered before morning.

"That evening his father and a number of other men were gathered together in the town hall of Lucerne to talk over community affairs, when Peter suddenly burst into the room, his eyes as big as saucers.

"The men gathered about him, thinking he must have some tremendous piece of news, but Peter spoke never a word to them. Instead, he marched up to the great porcelain stove that stood in the room.

"'O Stove,' said Peter, 'I have just heard terrible things which I have promised not to tell to a *living soul*, but you, O Stove, have no soul, so to you I will say that the Austrians are now in the tunnel underneath the walls and that at midnight they will break in and sack the town.'

"At first the men thought Peter had gone crazy, but when he had finished telling the stove all he had seen and heard, they flew to alarm the town and get their weapons.

"At midnight, when the Austrians came up through the hole in the stable floor, they were received by a little army of men of Lucerne, and in the battle that followed they were completely whipped and driven from the town forever. And it was Peter who saved the city.

"You see that was Peter's chance to show what he was made of, and he did n't miss his chance. He did the right thing, even though he was afraid. It's a great thing not to miss one's chance."

The old herdsman looked up at the moon as if he hadn't meant any one in particular when he said that about missing one's chance, and the children didn't say a word for a minute.

Then Seppi said, "If Peter could save a whole town, I guess we can get down that pass with a few goats."

"Why, of course," said the herdsman. "It's your chance, you see, and when you get home very likely you'll find you are both heroes. You see if there were never any danger, there never could be any heroes at all! Now climb up into the hay, both of you, and I'll wake you for an early start in the morning."

V
THE PASS

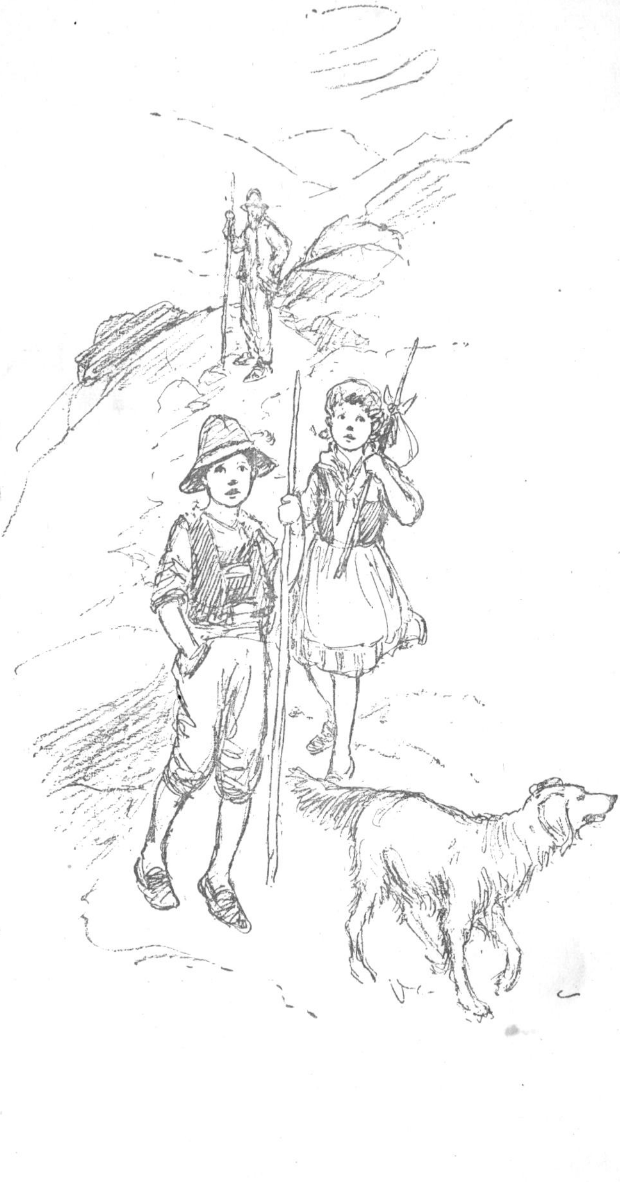

V

THE PASS

ALL night long the children slept soundly in the hayloft, with the moon peering in at them through the chinks between the logs. In the morning they were awakened by the music of cow-bells, and by the voice of the old herdsman, who stuck his head up through the hole in the floor and called out: "Wake up, my young heroes! The sun is already looking over the crest of Rigi, and it's time you were on your way."

Seppi and Leneli sat up and rubbed their eyes, and for a moment could not think where they were or how they came to be there. Then they remembered, and, springing from their rude beds, ran out into the glorious morning and washed their faces and hands in the mountain stream that flowed near the hut. Then there were the goats to be milked, and breakfast to be eaten, and the shadows were already shortening when at last they were ready for their lonely and dangerous journey.

The old herdsman packed some bread and cheese in their lunch-cloth, Leneli slung the bundle on her alpenstock, and Seppi called Bello to herd the goats. But the goats were well pleased with the rich green grass of the alp, and were unwilling to leave the pasture. They frisked and gamboled and stood on their hind legs butting each other playfully, and it was some time before Seppi and Bello could get them fairly started.

The old herdsman had done his milking very early in order to go a little way with the children, and now, leaving the cows in charge of his faithful dog, he led the way down the steep mountain path.

The morning air was so clear and sparkling and the sun shone so bright upon the snow-capped peaks, that the children almost forgot the dangers of the unknown path. It seemed impossible that anything could happen to them in such a wonderful and beautiful world, and they said good-bye quite cheerfully to the good old herdsman when at last he stopped and told them he must go back to his cheese-making. From the place where they stood, they could see the path like a tiny thread, winding through forests, down a long, narrow valley shut in by high cliffs, past waterfalls fed by mountain snows, and losing itself at last where a tiny white steeple marked the little village which was the home of the old herdsman. The old man pointed to it. "Follow the path and remember Peter of Lucerne," he said. "This is your chance! Trust the good God, do not be afraid, and soon your troubles will be over and you will be once more in your mother's arms." He stood on a rock and watched the little procession until a bend in the path hid it from sight, then he went back to his lonely pasture.

For an hour or so, the children trudged

quite cheerfully on their way. "This is n't hard at all," said Seppi. "The pass is easier to follow than our own. How silly we were to be scared!"

They were so used to climbing about in perilous places that when a little later the path led them along a shelf-like projection on the side of steep cliffs, overhanging a mountain stream, they were not frightened. But when they began to grow tired, and the trail led them into a dark forest, where the sun came through the thick boughs and shone only in patches of light upon the slippery spruce needles, they grew less courageous.

"I don't like the forest," said Leneli, shivering a little and looking behind her. "It always seems as if things would happen to you in the woods."

"What kind of things?" said Seppi, who was beginning to feel a bit shaky himself.

"Why—you know," answered Leneli, "the kind of things that giants and dragons and dwarfs do! And then there's that story about Pontius Pilate. You know our old

Mount Pilatus was named that because they say his body was thrown into one of its lakes, and his spirit haunts the mountain. He only comes out once a year, but oh, Seppi, suppose this should be the time!"

"Huh!" said Seppi scornfully. "Girls' talk! Of course I don't believe such things; besides, he only comes out on Good Friday, anyway!"

"Well," said Leneli, "lots of people do believe them, even grown-up people."

"Pooh," said Seppi, and just to show that he did n't care at all about such idle tales he began to whistle; but Leneli noticed that he too looked behind him now and then.

It grew more and more difficult to find the way, for there were openings between the trees that looked like paths and the true path wound in and out, and came near losing itself entirely among the rocks. The brown needles covered the ground in every direction, so the pass was no different in color from the rest of the forest floor. When they looked behind them or peered fearfully under the spruce boughs for dwarfs or giants, of course they were not watching the trail carefully, and so, when suddenly there was a loud whirring noise above the trees and a great bird flew almost over their heads, they were so startled they just ran without noticing which way they were going. Bello was startled too, and began to bark. This started the goats, and before you could say "Jack Robinson" children, dog, goats, and all were galloping pell-mell through the woods.

After the loud whirring noise the forest was still again, and the children stopped their mad race, but they could not stop the goats. On and on they ran with Bello after them, and there was nothing for the children to do but follow, for had not their father told them that the welfare of the whole family depended upon the goats, and if any should be lost, they alone would be to blame? Stumbling over roots, dodging trees and rocks, they plunged wildly along until finally they saw a light spot ahead and a moment later came out suddenly upon the edge of a precipice, from which they could look straight down into a deep valley below. The goats were there before them huddled together on the brow of the cliff, bleating piteously. Bello sat on his haunches with his tongue hanging out and looked at the scenery! Seppi and Leneli looked at each other in dismay.

"Now you've done it!" said Seppi miserably. "We've lost the path, and it's all your fault! If we had been thinking about Peter of Lucerne instead of about those silly old giants and dwarfs, this would not have happened."

"You were just as scared as I was," said Leneli, "and you need n't try to lay it all on me! You jumped and ran just as soon as I did, when that bird flew over our heads."

Seppi knew that this was true, so he said nobly: "Very well, let's not quarrel about it. What we need to do is to get the goats back to the path."

He took some salt from his pocket, as his big brother had taught him to do, and walked slowly toward them, holding out his hand. Nanni stretched her neck forward

and had taken just one lick of the salt when suddenly the loud whirring noise came again, there was a terrific scream overhead, and from the crags above them a great golden eagle swooped down towards the frightened group on the cliff, and, sticking his terrible talons into Nanni's back, tried to lift her bodily into the air! For an instant she swung dizzily over the edge of the cliff as the eagle beat his wings furiously in an effort to rise with his heavy burden. But in that instant Seppi leaped forward and, seizing the goat by the tail, pulled back with all his might. Leneli sprang to the rescue of Seppi, grasping him firmly around the waist, and screaming like a wildcat as she added her strength to his.

Meanwhile Bello barked furiously, and the rest of the goats fled bleating into the woods in a mad stampede. It was all over in less time that it takes to tell it. The goat, wounded and bleeding, dropped to the ground, the great bird soared away into the dizzy spaces beyond the cliff, and the children dashed into the shelter of the woods, dragging Nanni after them. They could not sink down on the ground and recover from their fright as they longed to do, for by this

time the goats had scattered among the trees and must be brought together again at once. Bello was distractedly trying to round them up, but as he had no idea of the direction in which to drive them, they were all galloping wildly about, first this way, then that.

It was some time before the children succeeded in getting the flock together again, but at last they were able to drive them farther into the woods, and away from the dangers of the cliffs, and were soon fortunate enough to come upon a little mountain stream which was singing its way through the forest. Here the goats stopped willingly to drink, and for the first time the children were able to give some attention to Nanni. Her back was torn and bloody, but her injuries were not serious and on the whole she seemed little the worse for her experience.

"We must let all the goats rest a little," said Seppi. "There isn't any food for them, but they can have a good drink while we eat our lunch, and then we just *must* find that path."

They sat down on a rock and Leneli opened the bundle of food which the old herdsman had given them. "Is n't it queer?" said she, as she handed Seppi a piece of cheese, "I 'm not as scared as I was before that dreadful eagle came. Are you?"

Seppi paused with his mouth open for a bite. "Why, I 'm not, either!" he said with surprise.

Leneli's eyes grew big. "Seppi," said she earnestly, "do you suppose, maybe, we 're heroes like Peter of Lucerne, after all, and never knew it?"

Seppi thought about this so seriously that for a minute he forgot to eat. Then he said, "Why, of course we are! We were scared but we did the right thing! My, but I'm glad!" He sighed with relief and took a big bite and munched away in silence.

At last he said solemnly, "Of course, now that we know we really are heroes, we won't be scared any more! We'll stop before we begin!"

Leneli looked doubtful. "I'm afraid I shall be scared again if we don't find the Pass," she said. "We might die up here in the mountains just like Moses in sight of the promised land. And some time maybe a hunter would find our bones lying scattered about on the ground." She sniffed a little at this pathetic picture, and her eyes filled with tears.

"Look here," said Seppi, jumping to his feet and gazing down at her sternly. "Is that any way for a hero to talk? They aren't going to find any bones of mine, I can tell you! I'm going to get down this mountain with all the goats, and so are you!"

"Well," said the heroine, doubtfully, "I was only supposing."

"Well, then, don't suppose that way," growled Seppi. "Just suppose we find the pass and get somewhere in time for supper, and get home to-morrow!"

At that very minute a bright thought struck him. "What a silly!" he said. "Why did n't I think of it before? This stream runs down hill, and if we follow it we shall have to get down to the valley, too. Come along!"

He was in such a hurry to carry out his idea that he started at once with his bread and cheese in his hand.

"But maybe it won't be anywhere near the village where the herdsman's home is, if we do get down," objected Leneli; "we ought to find the path."

"We'll be more likely to find it by following the stream," said Seppi, giving a loud blast on his horn, "and if we don't find that village, we'll find another place just as good. I'll bet there are some kind people everywhere."

Bello was at that moment barking down a hollow log in the hope of catching a hare, but he obediently rounded up the goats when Seppi called him, and the little caravan began to move.

It was not so simple as it sounded. The stream had worn a deep channel among the rocks. Trees had fallen across it, undermined by the swift current. Here it roared through a narrow gorge and there spread into a wide pool, then again plunged through underbrush and among rocks in its haste to reach the lake far below. The goats made slow progress and, whenever it was possible to do so, wandered away into easier paths and had to be driven back.

At last, to their great relief, the children saw a break in the trees, and they rushed joyfully forward, only to find that the stream at this point leaped over a cliff in a waterfall fifty feet high! The young explorers gazed at this new difficulty without a word.

Far below in the green valley they could see little white specks which were farm buildings, and tiny villages nestling among trees along the banks of a wide stream. They could even see the glacier which fed this river, lying like some huge white monster along the valley, its broad nose thrust between the banks on either side.

"Every time we think we've found the way out, we just get deeper in than ever," moaned Leneli, at last. "We can't get down this way, and if we did we'd have to cross the glacier."

"It isn't a very big one," said Seppi, looking down at it.

"You can't tell from here," quavered Leneli.

Seppi looked about him. To the right the forest slopes stretched upward toward the mountain-top. In front was the plunge, and at the left the stream gurgled over rocks and stones to its fall.

"We'll just have to cross it," said Seppi firmly. He drove the goats back a little way to a place where it was possible to ford the stream, and in a little while the whole caravan stood dripping on the farther bank.

"I 'm going to follow along the edge of this cliff," said Seppi, "and you and the goats follow after me. I 'm sure we shall find a place where we can get down. I 'll keep calling, so you 'll know which way to go."

He plunged into the forest at the word and was lost to sight, and Leneli, driving the goats before her, plunged after him. Guided by the sound of the waterfall, they forced their way through underbrush, over great piles of rocks and around perilous curves, seeking always the lower levels, until at last, when she was almost ready to give up in despair, Leneli heard a joyful shout from Seppi and, hastening forward, found him at the edge of the forest, looking out over a wide range of foothills. The forest was now behind them, and before them lay green slopes spangled like the stars in the milky way with yellow daffodils and blue gentians.

The goats, wild with delight at seeing fresh pasturage, leaped forward and began to browse, and dear old Bello sat down on his haunches with his tongue hanging out and gazed upon the scene as benevolently as if his own stomach were full instead of empty. The children were so weary they threw themselves down in the grass beside him to rest.

Now that they had escaped the perils of the forest, it almost seemed to them for a little while as if their troubles were over, but by and by Seppi sat up and studied the scene before them. He looked past the long slopes to the glacier and the river in the valley below.

"We've got to get across that somehow," he said to Leneli, at last, pointing to the stream, "and there are only two ways of doing it. When we get down there, we must either go through the river, or across the glacier which feeds it."

"We can't go through it," answered Leneli. "We don't know how deep it is."

"Then it will have to be the glacier," said Seppi, "and I'm glad goats are so sure-footed. We'd better start along, for it's getting later every minute, and I'm bound to reach that farm-house before dark." He pointed to a speck in the distance.

"Oh, dear," sighed Leneli, as she followed his finger with her eye, "it's like dying to get to heaven! Suppose we fall into cracks in the glacier?"

"You're the worst supposer I ever saw," snapped Seppi. "Suppose we don't fall in! Suppose we get across all right with all the goats, and suppose there's a good woman at the farm-house who feeds us, and Bello too! Suppose she gives us . . . what would you like best for supper, Leneli?"

"Oh!" cried Leneli, clasping her hands, "soup and pancakes!"

"Hurry up, then," said Seppi. "We shall surely never get them, nor anything else, by staying here."

Leneli struggled to her feet, and once more they moved forward. Half an hour of brisk walking brought them to the edge of the glacier, and here Seppi arranged their marching order.

"I'll go first," he said, "the same as a guide, then the goats, and then you and Bello. You must watch every step, and keep sticking in your alpenstock to be sure you are on solid ice. If you don't, you might strike a hollow place and fall through the crust."

"I'll be careful," said Leneli.

"All right, then! here we go!" said Seppi. "I can just smell those pancakes!" and with that he set out across the river of ice.

The children understood very well the dangers of the glaciers. It was not simply a frozen stream on which one might skate. It was a great slow-moving, grinding avalanche of ice and rocks, full of seams and cracks and holes, which was creeping steadily down the valley. The river formed by the melting snows, gushed forth from beneath it and rushed away to join the lake still far below.

Even the goats knew it was a perilous journey, and besides they were unwilling to leave the rich grass of the fields, so it was with some difficulty that they were finally driven forward upon the glacier. Seppi led the way, blowing on his little horn to encourage them, trying every step with his stick, and waiting for them to catch up before going farther. They were nearly half way across, when Seppi stopped and called to Leneli to stand still. There in front of him yawned a wide crevasse. The frozen river had cracked open, and if they went forward in a straight line they would plunge down into an ice prison from which they could never escape alive.

It was the hardest puzzle and the greatest danger they had met in their whole journey, and for a minute poor Seppi almost gave up in despair. He thought they would have to go back and try the river after all. Shouting to Leneli to keep the goats together if she could, he turned and made his way up-stream along the edge of the crevasse. It grew narrower as he followed it, and broke into a number of smaller cracks.

The only way to get to the other side was to follow along these smaller cracks where they made a crooked natural bridge across the chasm. Even Seppi's stout heart quailed a little as he gazed down into the depths of the huge rifts. The walls of ice gleamed with wonderful greens and blues, but he had no heart to admire the beautiful colors.

"Remember Peter of Lucerne, and come on," he shouted back to Leneli, and without another word started across the treacherous ice bridge. It made no difference whether she was frightened or not, Leneli simply had to follow him even though the goats, sure-footed as they were, shrank from the journey, and Bello hung back and whined.

"Follow exactly in my footsteps," shouted Seppi, and Leneli swallowed a lump in her throat, grasped her alpenstock more firmly and went forward.

"Don't look down into the hole! Look at the bridge across it!" shouted Seppi.

He stepped carefully forward, finding solid footing with his stick before each step, and in a short time stood safely on the other side of the chasm. There he waited and held his breath, while the goats picked their way daintily across the ice bridge after him, and when Leneli and Bello at last reached his side, he hugged them both for joy.

"There," he said, "there can't be anything worse than that, and we'll soon be on green grass again."

They passed other smaller crevasses, but they could make their way around the ends of these, and it was not long before they had scrambled over the rocks at the glacier's edge and once more stood on solid ground. Even Bello seemed to realize that their troubles were now nearly over, for he barked and ran round them in circles and leaped up with his paws on their shoulders to give them dog kisses, and, as for his tail — he nearly wagged it loose in his joy. The goats sprang forward to reach the grass, and when the children drove them on, snatched greedy mouthfuls as they passed. The children could see the farm-house growing from a mere speck larger and larger as they came down the valley toward it, and at last the little group of stragglers pattered into the door-yard.

The noise of bleating goats and a barking dog brought the farmer's wife to the door, and for a moment she stood there with her baby in her arms and looked down at them in astonishment, just as the old herdsman had done on the mountain.

"Where in the world did you come from?" she cried at last. "Who are you? and what do you want here?"

Leneli opened her mouth to answer, but when she saw the woman's kind face, and the baby sucking its thumb and looking at them solemnly, it reminded her so of her mother and Baby Roseli that, instead of explaining, she burst into tears.

The woman clattered down the steps at

once, put her free arm around Leneli, and patted her comfortingly, while Seppi told her their story. Before he had got farther than the avalanche part of it, she seemed to guess all the rest. It was not the first time that people had been lost on the mountain.

"Come right in this minute," she cried. "Don't stop to talk! You must be as hungry as wolves. I'll get you something to eat, and then you can tell me every word."

"Please," said Leneli timidly, drying her tears, "could you give Bello something first? The goats have had a little grass and we had some bread and cheese, but Bello hasn't had a bite all day."

"Bless my soul!" said the woman. "What a little woman it is, to think first of the dog! Here," she cried to Seppi; "take this bone to him right away, and shut up the goats in the barn-yard. Then come back and I'll give you whatever you like best, if I've got it!"

"If you please, ma'am," said Seppi, his eyes shining, "up on the mountain when we were lost, we saw your house and we just supposed that maybe you might have soup and pancakes!"

"Bless my soul!" cried the woman. "Soup and pancakes it shall be, and that's soon ready!"

She put the baby into Leneli's arms and

flew about the kitchen, rattling pots and pans, stirring up the fire, and mixing her batter; and when Seppi returned, the smell of pancakes was already in the air, and the soup was bubbling in the pot. In five minutes more the children were seated at the kitchen table with steaming bowls before them, while their new friend cooked a pile of pancakes that it would have warmed the cockles of your heart to see.

The farmer himself was far away on the high alps with his cattle, and came down the mountain only once in a while with a load of cheeses on his back. His wife was very lonely in his absence and was glad to have company, if only for a single night; so she comforted the children and talked with them about their mother, and piled pancakes on their plates until they could not hold another mouthful. Then she helped them milk the goats, and when the sun went down, sent them to bed so they would be well rested for their long walk the next day.

VI
NEW FRIENDS AND OLD

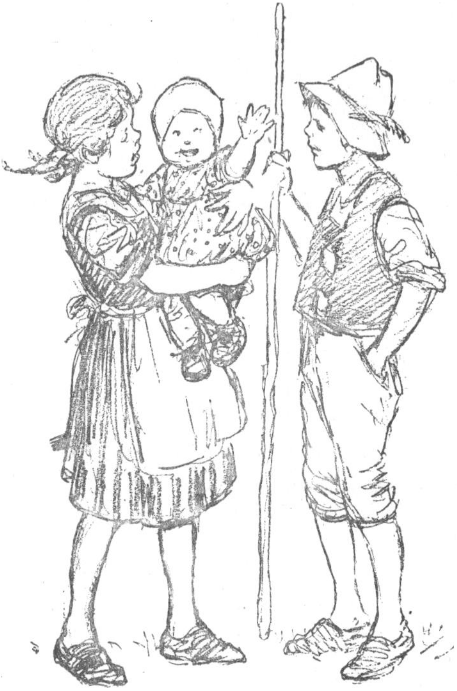

VI
NEW FRIENDS AND OLD

When the children came into the kitchen the next morning, they found their new friend beating mush and milk together for their breakfast, and there was a smell of coffee in the air.

"Sit right down and eat," said she, pushing a stool toward the table with her foot. "I've milked the goats for you. They did n't give much, poor things, and it's no wonder, after such a day as they had yesterday! The wonder is that they gave any at all. I've made coffee for you, for you've a long day ahead of you, and it will cheer up your insides. It's a lucky thing for you the day is so fine. I thought I heard it rain in the night, but old Pilatus' head has no cloud cap this morning, and he is a good weather prophet."

The baby was already seated in her high chair at the table, beating upon it with a spoon to welcome them, and the children were soon seated beside her putting away a great store of the good mush. The farmer's wife had no one but the baby to talk to during the long days when her husband was away, and she made the most of her time while the children were with her. She told them all about her cows and her pigs and her chickens, just how much hay her husband brought down from his highland meadow on his back the previous summer, and how many cheeses he expected to bring home from the alp at the end of the season. And when at last they had eaten all they could, she put up a lunch for them, and gave them full directions for reaching their own village.

"It's not hard at all," said she, "for though it is still a long way to the foot of the mountain, you've only to follow the road, and if you don't know which turn to take at a cross-roads, there'll always be somebody to ask somewhere along the way. If you could get so far down the mountain and across the glacier by yourselves you 've nothing to fear now, and you 'd better make all the speed you can, for my heart bleeds for your poor mother. She must be half dead with anxiety by now."

She kissed them good-bye at the door and stood with her baby on her arm, gazing after them when they drove the goats out of the door-yard and started down the highway toward their home. They did not forget to thank their kind hostess, and after they had started turned again and again to wave a farewell to her. She waved to them in return, and the baby also fluttered her tiny pink hand until they were quite out of sight.

"We 'll never forget her, shall we?" said Leneli.

"Never," answered Seppi, fervently. "She 's almost as good as Mother! And does n't she make good pancakes, though?"

They set their faces northward and

trudged along, hurrying rather than slacking their speed as the miles lengthened behind them, for as the distance between them and their home shortened, their eagerness to get there increased. It was a good twelve miles from the farm-house where they had spent the night to their own village, and a mile this side of the village and a mile up the mountain-slope was their own dear home. This, to the sturdy Swiss boy and girl, brought up in the mountains, was not a hard walk, but they knew that goats must not be driven too fast if they are expected to give any milk, so it was late afternoon before the cavalcade reached the foot of their own hill-side and began the last climb of the weary journey.

The children could see their own roof, weighted down by stones, peeping over the edge of the hill long before they were anywhere near it, and they fastened their homesick eyes upon it as a sailor fixes his upon the North Star at sea. Now they could see the whole house, with the goat-shed and cow-stables back of it, the straw-stack, and the southern slope of the garden.

They strained their eyes for a glimpse of their mother, but there was no movement to be seen anywhere about the place. Even the breeze had died down, so there was not so much as a flutter among the trees as they drew nearer and nearer. At last, unable to hold themselves back longer, they broke into a run and came dashing into the yard with all the goat-bells jingling, Bello barking, and their own voices raised in a joyful shout: "Mother, Mother, where are you? We're home!"

But to their surprise and great disappointment, there was no answer. The house was as still as if it were asleep. Leaving the goats to Bello, the children dashed into the kitchen. There was no one there, and there was no sound but the loud tick-tock of the cuckoo clock. They dashed upstairs to the bedrooms and back again to the kitchen. Everywhere silence.

"It's just as if the house were dead when

Mother is n't in it," sobbed Leneli. "Where can she be? And Roseli too!"

"Roseli is where Mother is, you may be sure," said Seppi.

They ran outdoors again, and found Bello barking madly at Nanni, who was having a blissful time with the carrot-tops, which she refused to leave even when Bello, who knew very well she should n't be in the garden at all, nipped at her heels.

"We 'll have to shut up the goats," said Seppi, as he ran to Bello's assistance.

They drove them into the shed, gave them some hay, and then rested their weary legs for a moment, sitting on the kitchen steps, while they considered what to do next.

Then an awful thought struck Leneli. "The avalanche!" she gasped. "Maybe she was caught by it!"

Seppi grew pale and gulped down a sob. "No," he said, when after a moment he could speak. "I don't believe it! There's no sign of the avalanche about here, and

Mother never goes away from home. She's trying to find us; that's what she's doing!"

Leneli collapsed on the step. "Oh, Seppi," she cried, "do you suppose she's lost on the mountain just as we've found ourselves and got home again?" The thought was too much for her, and she sobbed afresh.

"Well," said Seppi, "crying won't do any good. Let's go and see if we can find her."

Weary as they were, they started at once to their feet to begin this new quest, even though the shadows were long across the flower-starred mountain-slopes and the sun was already sinking toward the west.

As they rounded the corner of the house, Seppi gave a joyful shout and pointed up the goat-path toward the mountain. There, a long distance off, they saw their mother coming toward them with Baby Roseli in her arms! Even at that distance they could see that she looked weary and sad, for her head drooped and her step was slow.

All their own weariness vanished like

magic at sight of her, and with a shout that waked the echoes on old Pilatus they bounded up the path to meet her.

She heard the shout, and, shading her eyes with her hand, looked eagerly in the direction of the sound, and in another minute mother and children were clasped in each other's arms, while Baby Roseli crowed with delight from a nest in the midst of grass and flowers where she had been suddenly deposited.

For a moment they gave themselves up to the joy of reunion, then Seppi said proudly: "We brought the goats safely home, Mother. They are all in the shed."

"I thought you had been swallowed up by the avalanche," sobbed their mother, clasping them again to her heart. "All the men of the village are now up the mountain-side searching for you and trying to break a fresh path to the goat-pastures. They must be told that you are safe."

She sprang to her feet, and started back up the path. Then she thought of Seppi's horn. "Blow," she cried, "blow Fritz's tune if you can. They all know it, and some of them are near enough to hear."

Seppi put the horn to his lips and blew. At first it was only a dismal squawk; then, though it sounded much like the crowing of a young rooster in imitation of an old one, he did manage to achieve the first few notes of Fritz's tune. Soon a head appeared above a rock far up the trail, then a whole man scrambled to the top of it and gazed earnestly at the little group in the path below.

Again Seppi sounded his horn, his mother flung out her apron like a flag of victory, and all of them, including Roseli, waved their arms so joyously that there was no mistaking the message. With an answering shout the man dropped out of sight again behind the rock, and a few moments later they saw him running down the hillside toward the village.

Soon the church-bell was clanging joyfully from the belfry, carrying the news of the wanderers' safe return to every one within hearing distance. Bells from the adjoining village joined the clamor, and horns answering from distant crags told the glad news. The toilers on the mountain-side heard and rejoiced.

From the cliffs where the echoes lived came shout after shout, and soon the women of the village, who had been watching with the distracted mother and helping in the work of the men, came hurrying down the goat-path to welcome the wanderers and rejoice over their safe return. They were joined by one and another of the men as they returned from the mountain-side, until quite a group had gathered in the blossoming field to hear the children tell the story of their perilous adventures. They were standing thus when the sun dipped behind the western hills and the Angelus once more called the countryside to prayer. With grateful hearts and bowed heads, neighbors and friends gave thanks to God for his mercies, then scattered to their own firesides, leaving the happy mother and children together.

When they entered the kitchen of the old farm-house once more, the tiny wooden cuckoo hopped out of his tiny wooden door and shouted "cuckoo" seven times, and when they had eaten their supper, and the children sat beside the great stove telling their mother all over again about the old herdsman, and the eagle, and the farmer's wife, and all the other events of their three days on the mountain, the cuckoo waited fifteen whole minutes beyond the hour before he could make up his mind to remind them of bed-time. Then he stuck his head out once more and cried "cuckoo" quite hysterically eight times. Even then they lingered to talk about Father and Fritz far away in the high alps, and of how glad they were that they knew nothing of the dangers and anxieties they had just been through.

"Dear me!" said the mother, rising at last, "how fast the time goes when we are happy! It's long past your bed hour, and you must be very tired. We must stop talking this very minute!"

She sent the children upstairs, tucked them in bed, heard their prayers, and kissed them good-night. Then she came back to the kitchen, patted Bello, who was sound asleep on the doorstep, looked at the moon rising over the crest of Rigi, fastened the door, pulled up the weights to wind the clock, and, taking her candle, went upstairs to bed herself.

When at last the sound of her footsteps ceased, and the house was quiet for the night, the cuckoo stuck out his head and looked about the silent kitchen. The moonlight streamed in at the eastern window, the little mouse was creeping from her hole, and the shadows were whispering together in corners.

"On the whole," said the cuckoo to himself, "I think I've managed this thing very well. Every one is happy again, and now I can take a little rest myself. The past three days have been very wearying to one with my responsibilities."

"Cuckoo," he called nine times, then the tiny wooden door clapped shut, and he too went to sleep.

SUGGESTIONS TO TEACHERS

CHILDREN are intensely interested in the life of children in other lands; and from this book they will learn much about how little people live in Switzerland — perhaps the most picturesque and appealing of the countries of Europe.

Journey geography. In geography for the fourth grade much emphasis is properly placed on imaginary journeys. By using the Swiss Twins in connection with wall maps, steamship folders, and geography texts, a series of journeys to Switzerland may be taken. Following is a suggestive series of journey lessons.

1. *Getting acquainted with new friends, the Swiss twins.* Chapter I. This might be a reading lesson, or read as a treat, by the teacher.

2. *A trip to visit Seppi and Leneli in their Swiss home.* Plan the trip with the aid of maps and pictures. Let the children choose the route. If other countries en route have already been studied, a good opportunity is here offered for review of the sights to be seen on the way. The aim of the lesson should be to teach that Switzerland is a mountainous land far from the sea. Following the lesson the children should make a collection of pictures of mountains, particularly the Alps.

3. *Helping Leneli and Seppi take the goats to the high pasture.* Chapter II should be read in connection with this lesson. Emphasize milking the goats, the cattle taken to the high Alps, cheese-making, the mountainside garden, the long climb, and views of distant snow-clad peaks.

4. *Cattle on the high Alps.* Chapters III and IV might well be read in connection with lessons in reading, spelling, and composition. Opportunity for a good geography lesson is given by an imaginary trip with Fritz and his father to the high Alps with the cattle. Discuss why this trip is necessary, the value of cheese-making, what becomes of the cheeses.

5. *The Twins' adventure; the avalanche*. Following the reading of the story the children might dramatize the adventure. Included should be the idea of the avalanche, how it is caused, how houses are protected against it, the damage done. Glaciers may be emphasized at the same time.

6. *The return journey*. Let another route be chosen. Let each child bring home a souvenir, and on the steamer read aloud parts of the diary kept during the visit.

Problems. In the geography for the upper grades, much emphasis has recently been placed on teaching by problems. Just as much opportunity is offered in the fourth grade to use simple problems to motivate the lesson. The younger children are, however, more interested in the "how" than the "why": —

1. "How do the Swiss goats get their food?" 2. "How does Father earn the living for the Twins and the rest of the family?" 3. "How does Bello the dog help the family?" 4. "Why are the Swiss mountain-tops covered with snow and ice?" 5. "Why do avalanches start?"

Projects. The Swiss Twins offers splendid opportunities for "projects," activities that children eagerly undertake. A few are suggested below: —

1. *The Twins and their home*. Have the children dress tiny dolls as the Twins. Lucy Fitch Perkins's illustrations give every needed suggestion. The house can be made of cardboard, painted or covered with split-pencil slabs. See the picture on page 36 and the description on page 122. The mountains may be modelled in clay or cut from cardboard and painted. The cattle and goats may be made of plastecene, cardboard, or wool on a cardboard foundation. In such a project, the ingenuity of the whole class will produce on the sand table a product to be proud of.

2. *A collection of Swiss objects*. One part of the schoolroom may be set aside as a museum. Toys, pictures, carved objects, embroideries, dresses, watches, — the collection will grow apace. The children would enjoy acting as hosts and guides on a day set aside for mothers and other interested visitors.

3. *Pictures of Switzerland*. The descriptions in the

Swiss Twins will suggest pictures to be brought from home to adorn the schoolroom. Post cards, and the files of the National Geographic Magazine will furnish abundant material. A simple stencil may be made to decorate the blackboard border with mountain scenes, the chalking to be done, of course, by the children.

Dramatization. Whatever makes vivid the life of the children of Switzerland is good geography. Perhaps nothing appeals more to children than simple dramatization. The Swiss Twins is full of suggestions; for example: —
Chapter I. *The Angelus; Putting baby Roseli to sleep.* — Chapter II. *What happened to the lunch.* — Chapter III. *The blocked path; The story of Peter of Lucerne.* — Chapter V. *Crossing the glacier.* — Chapter VI. *The home coming.*

BOOKS ABOUT SWITZERLAND

For Teachers: —
AUVERGNE's Switzerland in Sunshine and Snow. (Colored Illustrations.)
CADBY's Switzerland in Winter.
DOLE's The Spell of Switzerland.
GERBER's Switzerland Illustrated.
HUG and STEAD's The Story of Switzerland.
MCKENZIE's Switzerland.
ROOK's Switzerland, the Country and Its People. (Colored Illustrations.)
TAPPAN's The Netherlands and Switzerland. In The World's Story, Vol. 7.
WEBB's Switzerland and the Swiss.
ANONYMOUS. Switzerland and the Swiss.

For Pupils:
FROELICHER's Swiss Stories and Legends.
GEORGE's A Little Journey to France and Switzerland.
MIRICK and HOLMES's Home Life Around the World, Chapter VI.
STEVENSON's Children's Classics in Dramatic Form, Book IV.
SPYRI's Heidi; Chel; Moni the Goat Boy; The Story of Rico.
TAPPAN's Old World Hero Stories, Chapter XXXVII.